# Volcanoes & Earthquakes

This 2005 edition published by
The Book People
by arrangement with
Weldon Owen Pty Ltd

ISBN 1-74089-373-5
Colour reproduction by
Colourscan Overseas Co Pte Ltd
Printed by SNP Leefung Printers

Printed in China

# Volcanoes &
# Earthquakes

CONSULTING EDITOR

### Dr Eldridge M. Moores
Professor of Geology
University of California at Davis, California

WELDON OWEN

# Contents

## • EARTHQUAKES •

## FAMOUS VOLCANOES •

## • FAMOUS EARTHQUAKES •

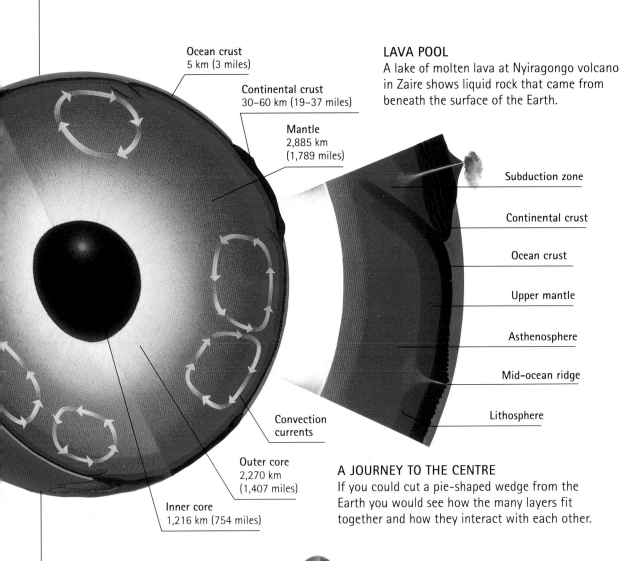

Ocean crust
5 km (3 miles)

Continental crust
30–60 km (19–37 miles)

Mantle
2,885 km
(1,789 miles)

Convection
currents

Outer core
2,270 km
(1,407 miles)

Inner core
1,216 km (754 miles)

**LAVA POOL**
A lake of molten lava at Nyiragongo volcano
in Zaire shows liquid rock that came from
beneath the surface of the Earth.

Subduction zone

Continental crust

Ocean crust

Upper mantle

Asthenosphere

Mid-ocean ridge

Lithosphere

**A JOURNEY TO THE CENTRE**
If you could cut a pie-shaped wedge from the
Earth you would see how the many layers fit
together and how they interact with each other.

• THE UNSTABLE EARTH •

# Fire Down Below

The Earth is made up of several layers. If you could stand at the
centre, 6,371 km (3,950 miles) down, you would see the solid iron
inner core, which is surrounded by an outer core of liquid iron
and nickel. To travel to the surface, you would pass through the solid
rock of the lower mantle, then the soft, squishy area of rock called the
asthenosphere. The final two layers join together to form the lithosphere,
which is made up of the solid rock of the upper mantle, and the crust.
The crust covers the Earth as thin apple peel covers an apple. Inside the
Earth, radioactive elements decay and produce heat, and the temperature
increases to an amazing 3,000°C (5,432°F) at the core. This heat provides
the energy for the layers to move and interact. Melted rock called magma
rises from deep within the Earth to near the surface. Some of it cools and
becomes solid within the crust but some erupts on the surface as lava.

6

Philippine plate

Eurasian plate

North American plate

Cocos plate

Pacific plate

African plate

South American plate

Indo-Australian plate

Caribbean plate

Nazca plate

Antarctic plate

## THE CHANGING EARTH
For nearly one billion years continents have bunched together and spread apart in the very slow but continuing movement of the plates.

500 million years ago

325–350 million years ago

Pangaea the supercontinent
200 million years ago

Pangaea splits into
Gondwana and Laurasia
130 million years ago

Gondwana and Laurasia
65 million years ago

• THE UNSTABLE EARTH •

# The Moving Continents

The Earth's outermost section, the lithosphere, is separated into seven large and several small jagged slabs called lithospheric plates, which fit together much like puzzle pieces. The crust or top part of each two-layered plate comes from either an ocean, a continent or a bit of both. You cannot feel it but the plates are constantly moving. Supported by the soft, squishy material of the asthenosphere under them, plates pull and push against each other at a rate of 2–20 cm ($^3$/$_4$–8 in) per year. When plates pull apart, magma from the mantle erupts and forms new ocean crust. When they move together, one plate slowly dives under the other and forms a deep ocean trench. Mountain ranges form when some plates collide. Other plates slide and scrape past each other. Most volcanoes and earthquakes occur along edges where plates meet.

ALFRED WEGENER 1880 1930
GRÖNLAND FORSCHER
S4
REPUBLIK ÖSTERREICH

### A NEW THEORY
In 1915, Alfred Wegener, a German scientist and explorer, proposed his theory of continental drift. He wrote of a huge supercontinent, Pangaea, which split apart millions of years ago. The pieces then slowly drifted to their present position. Not until the mid-1960s was the theory revised and accepted by scientists.

Mid-ocean mountains
The longest mountain range in the world is the gently sloping mid-ocean ridge system, which snakes along the ocean floor at the boundaries of the plates.

## STRANGE BUT TRUE

Many millions of years ago, the east coast of South America and the west coast of Africa fitted together as part of the same landmass. Today, the two continents even have similar rock, plant and animal fossils.

*Glossopteris*

## SLIDING BY

When some plates meet they slide past each other in opposite directions or in the same direction at different speeds. The edges of the sliding plates grind when they meet causing a series of weblike cracks or faults and fractures to occur. Here an orchard changes course to follow the line of a fault—a simple example of plate movement. As the two plates move slowly past each other stress builds up in the rocks below and an earthquake can occur.

*Discover more in* Fire Down Below

# Ridges and Rift Valleys

The ocean crust is rugged with mountain ridges and deep rift valleys or cracks. When two plates with ocean crust move apart, magma from the mantle bubbles up to the surface to fill the rift. The magma cools and hardens and adds new strips of crust or ocean floor to the edges of the two plates. This forms what is called a spreading or widening ridge. The Atlantic Ocean is widening by 2 cm (3/4 in) per year. The East Pacific Rise is widening by 20 cm (8 in) per year—the fastest widening rate of an ocean floor. In 10 million years, it will be 2,000 km (1,240 miles) wider. Plates continue to move away from the spreading ridge towards other plates. When a spreading ridge fractures or breaks, earthquakes occur. Mid-ocean ridge volcanoes also form in rifts, fed by the magma from below. Over millions of years, they can grow so large that they rise above the water to form islands such as Iceland on the North Atlantic mid-ocean ridge.

**Smoking chimneys**
Sulphur and other minerals deposited on the sides of the vents build natural chimneys of up to 10 m (33 feet).

## SEA FLOOR SPREADING
New lithospheric plate is created at a spreading ridge.

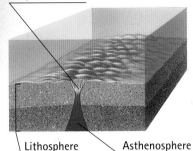

Magma chamber

Lithosphere    Asthenosphere

As two plates with ocean crust move apart, a crack or rift forms.

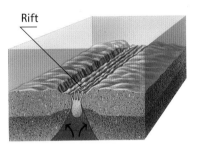

Rift

Magma from the mantle rises to fill the rift between the two plates.

Magma cools and hardens, and adds to the edges of the plates.

## BLACK SMOKERS
Volcanic hot springs or hydrothermal vents such as these were discovered in 1977 and are found along very active spreading ridges on the ocean floor. The mineral-rich water is eaten by bacteria, which is food for other vent animals such as tube worms, giant clams and eelpouts.

**Circulation system**
The arrows show how cold sea water seeps down through the ridge. Magma heats it to an amazing 300°C (572°F), then the water rises back up through the vent.

## AN ISLAND IS BORN

In 1963, an undersea volcanic eruption created Surtsey Island, the newest landmass on Earth. Surtsey lies off the southwest coast of Iceland, a country known for its many active volcanoes. The eruption began with a large column of ash and smoke. Heat and pressure from deep within the Earth pushed part of the mid-Atlantic ridge to the surface. The island continued to grow for several months. Today, Surtsey Island measures 2.6 sq km (1 sq mile). Its dominant feature is the steep cone of the volcano.

*Discover more in* The Moving Continents

# Subduction

When two plates move towards each other and meet, one plate slowly dives or subducts beneath the other along what is called a subduction zone. This is an area of intense earthquake and volcanic activity caused by the movement of the two plates. There are three types of plate boundary where subduction occurs: ocean to ocean, ocean to continent and continent to continent. The action of subduction is the same for all three types but the results are different. The area at which one plate dives beneath another creates an ocean trench, the deepest part of the ocean floor. As the down-going plate continues to sink deeper into the mantle, it mixes with hot rock and melts to form magma. Under extreme heat and pressure, this new magma mixture then forces its way back upwards to erupt violently at the surface. Compared to the gentle chain of mid-ocean ridge volcanoes, subduction volcanoes are explosive and dangerous. This is due to the presence of water and the build-up of gases dissolved in the thick and sticky magma that is produced in the process of subduction.

## OCEAN TO OCEAN

When two plates with ocean crust meet, one plate subducts. When the magma rises to the surface it forms an island arc volcano chain such as the Lesser Antilles in the East Caribbean.

Island arc volcano

Ocean crust

Magma

Subduction zone

Asthenosphere

## OCEAN TO CONTINENT

When a plate with thin ocean crust meets a plate with thicker continental crust, the thinner plate subducts. Magma rises to the surface and forms a line of volcanoes such as these on the west coast of South America.

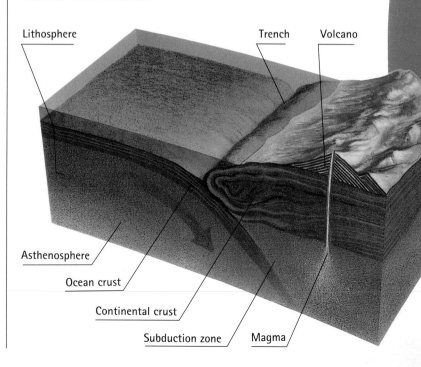

Lithosphere

Trench

Volcano

Asthenosphere

Ocean crust

Continental crust

Subduction zone

Magma

Trench · Ocean crust · Lithosphere

## RING OF FIRE

The Pacific Ring of Fire is the name scientists use to describe the area of the world located around the edges of the Pacific Ocean. This is actually the boundary of the large Pacific plate, which is slowing moving and subducting under or grinding past other plates it meets. In 1994, two volcanoes, Mt Tavurvur and Mt Vulcan, erupted in Rabaul, Papua New Guinea. These island arc volcanoes formed at an area where the Pacific plate is subducting under the South Bismarck ocean plate.

### WHERE IN THE WORLD?
This map shows the general locations in the world where one plate is subducting under another.

### CONTINENT TO CONTINENT
When these plates move towards each other, the thin ocean part of one plate subducts but the continental part continues to push against the other plate and forms a mountain chain such as the Himalayan Mountains in central Asia.

Mountains · Subduction zone · Continental crust · Lithosphere

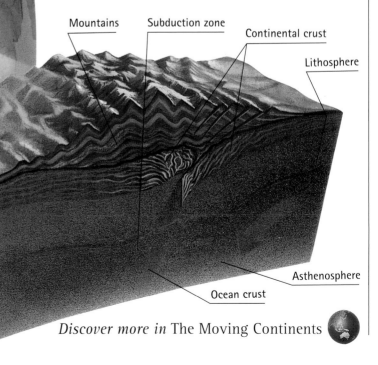

Asthenosphere · Ocean crust

*Discover more in* The Moving Continents

13

North American plate

Pacific plate

**WHERE IN THE WORLD?**
This map shows the locations of most of the world's hotspots.

**DIRECTION OF PLATES**
The Pacific plate, moving northwest, has slowly carried the oldest of the Hawaiian Islands away from the hotspot and closer to the point where they will subduct under the North American plate.

• THE UNSTABLE EARTH •

# Hotspots

Volcanoes are born in different ways and hotspot volcanoes, though spectacular, are often less violent than those that occur at subduction zones. Hotspot volcanoes form in the middle of plates, directly above a source of magma. Molten rock rises to the surface from deep within the Earth's mantle, pierces the plate like a blow torch and erupts in a lava flow or fountain. A hotspot stays still, but the plate keeps moving. Over millions of years this process forms a string of volcanic islands such as the Hawaiian Island chain on the Pacific plate. Hawaii's Mauna Loa and Kilauea, now active volcanoes, will gradually become dormant or cold as Hawaii moves off the hotspot. A new active volcano, such as Loihi to the southeast, might become a new island above the hotspot. The Pacific plate has carried other island volcanoes in the chain far away from the magma source.

**INDIAN OCEAN VOLCANO**
Piton de la Fournaise on Réunion Island is one of the most active volcanoes in the world.

14

## KILAUEA FLOWS

The lava that erupts from hotspot volcanoes such as Kilauea in Hawaii can move at speeds of up to 100 km (62 miles) per hour.

## HOTSPOT, CONTINENTAL STYLE

Yellowstone National Park, in the state of Wyoming in the United States, has spectacular geysers and natural hot springs, and is one of the most famous hotspots found on a continent. Underground water is heated by a hotspot source of magma deep within the mantle. The steam in the boiling water expands, and water and steam burst through the many cracks in the crust and erupt as geysers. Some scientists believe that one day, in the next few hundred thousand years, a major volcanic eruption could occur in the area.

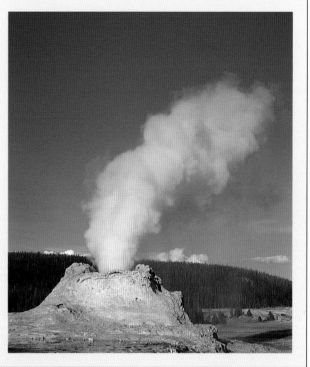

**Hawaii**
Kilauea and Mauna Loa are both volcanoes on the island of Hawaii.

**Loihi seamount**

## ASSEMBLY LINE ISLANDS

The Hawaiian Islands on the Pacific plate formed one by one above a hotspot or magma plume.

Lithosphere

Magma plume

In Kamchatka, Siberia, there is an old story about how a god named Tuli carries the Earth on a sled pulled by flea-ridden dogs. Whenever the dogs stop to scratch, the Earth shakes.

**ACCORDING TO LEGEND**
The ancient Greeks thought that Hephaistos, the god of fire, lived beneath Mt Etna in Sicily where he made weapons for the gods. When he beat the red-hot iron, fire leapt out of the volcano above.

• THE UNSTABLE EARTH •

# Myths and Legends

For thousands of years different cultures have told similar tales of powerful forces and superhuman gods to explain volcanic eruptions or earthquakes. Many myths blame these events on the anger of the gods or evil demons that live in volcanoes and from time to time punish their human subjects. The ancient Greeks thought that a volcano destroyed the island of Atlantis because its people became too wealthy and proud. The ancient Romans believed that their god of fire, Vulcan, lived and stoked his blacksmith furnace in a workshop beneath the present-day island of Vulcano. Hundreds of years ago, the Aztecs of Mexico and the people of Nicaragua believed gods lived in the lava lakes. They sacrificed beautiful young girls to these powerful gods.

## STRANGE BUT TRUE

In 1660, little black crosses rained down on the people of Naples—proof to many that St Januarius was looking after them. The crosses were really twinned pyroxene crystals, which the Mt Vesuvius volcano had hurled out of its crater.

## PELÉ

Pelé, the Hawaiian goddess of fire and volcanoes, supposedly lives in the crater of Kilauea volcano on Hawaii. She is thought to be responsible for the many volcanic eruptions on the island. In ancient times Pelé was greatly feared as she destroyed villages with her lava. Today she is still very much a part of Hawaiian folklore. Pelé has a terrible temper and she throws lava at anyone who speaks out against her. Pelé is also angered by anyone who steals her lava. Some people have been known to send back lava samples they have taken from the Hawaii Volcanoes National Park because of the bad luck they associate with an angry Pelé. There are also stories of lava flows avoiding the homes of people who loudly declared their trust in her. Many people claim to have seen Pelé before a volcanic eruption when she appears as a wrinkled old woman or a beautiful young girl. Others say they see her image in the glow of an eruption.

### A BALANCING ACT
According to an ancient Hindu myth, the Earth is carried on the back of an elephant, which stands on a turtle that is balanced on a cobra. Whenever one moves, the Earth trembles and shakes.

## TYPES OF VOLCANIC ERUPTION

### HAWAIIAN
Large amounts of runny lava erupt and produce large, low volcanoes.

### PELÉEAN
Blocks of thick sticky lava are followed by a burning cloud of ash and gas.

### STROMBOLIAN
Small sticky lava bombs and blocks, ash, gas and glowing cinders erupt.

### VULCANIAN
Violent explosions shoot out very thick lava and large lava bombs.

### PLINIAN
Cinders, gas and ash erupt great distances into the air.

# Volcanic Eruptions

Deep inside the Earth, magma rises upwards, gathers in pools within or below the crust and tries to get to the surface. Cracks provide escape routes and the magma erupts as a volcano. Steam and gas form clouds of white smoke, small fragments of rock and lava blow out as volcanic ash and cinder, and small hot bombs of lava shoot out and harden. Not all lava is the same. It may be thick and sticky or thin and runny. Lava thickness or viscosity determines the type of volcanic eruption and the kind of rock that forms when the lava hardens. Some volcanoes are active, erupting at any time; some are dormant or cold, waiting to erupt; others are dead or extinct. Volcanoes have shaped many of the Earth's islands, mountains and plains. They have also been responsible for changing weather, burying cities and killing people who live nearby.

### THE INSIDE STORY
This cross-section shows the inner workings of a volcano and what happens during an eruption.

### Side vent
Under pressure, this side vent branches off from the central vent and carries lava upwards through cracks in the rocks to ooze out the side of the volcano.

## WHY PEOPLE LIVE NEAR VOLCANOES

For centuries communities have grown up in the shadows of volcanoes. In Iceland, people use the energy from their island's many volcanoes to provide heat and power. Other people live near volcanoes because the soil is rich and farmers grow crops and graze their herds on the slopes. In Indonesia more people live on the islands with active volcanoes than on the islands with none. Shown here are lush rice terraces growing on the fertile ground near the volcano Mt Agung in Bali, Indonesia.

**From the top**
A white, smokelike mixture of steam, ash and gas is blown into the air. Hard bits of lava called bombs shoot out from the top while molten lava flows down the sides of the volcano.

**Crater**
This funnel-shaped opening at the top of the volcano enables lava, ash, gas and steam to erupt.

**Cone**
The cup-shaped cone is built up by ash and lava from a number of eruptions.

**Central vent**
The main vent or chimney rises from the magma chamber below. Magma flows up the vent to erupt on the surface as lava.

**Sill**
Magma does not always find an outlet to the surface. Some gathers, cools and becomes solid between two underground layers of rock.

**Magma chamber**
Thick molten magma travels upwards from the mantle and collects in large pockets in the crust where it mixes with gases and water. Under pressure from heat in the mantle the magma forces its way through vents to the surface.

**Fissure eruption**
Some magma forces its way upwards through vertical cracks in the rock and erupts on the surface.

**LAVA LAKES**
Lava collects in a series of pools after the eruption of Pu'u O'o in Hawaii.

**INTO THE SEA**
Runny lava gushes from the side of a Hawaiian volcano into the sea below, where it cools.

# Lava Flows

Lava is red-hot magma that erupts at the Earth's surface. A river of runny lava flows downhill from a volcano's central crater or oozes from a crack in the ground. It cools down from temperatures of up to 1,200°C (2,192°F), becomes stickier and slower-moving and often forms volcanic rock called basalt. Explosive, killer subduction volcanoes erupt thick, sticky lava that contains large amounts of silica. This cools to form rocks such as rhyolite, and different forms of volcanic glass such as obsidian. Large amounts of gas or water in the lava or a blocked outlet cause violent eruptions, with lava bombs and boulders shooting out in all directions. If lava hardens with a rough, broken surface, it is called aa. Lava that hardens with a smoother covering skin is called pahoehoe. Pahoehoe can wrinkle to form ropes of rock. Hardened lava often cracks to form regular columns.

## TYPES OF LAVA FLOW

Lava is named according to how it looks as it cools and hardens. Pillow lava is the most common form of lava found on Earth. It erupts in water especially along the mid-ocean ridge where volcanoes gently ooze pillow-shaped lumps of lava through cracks in the ocean floor. Pillow lava can also be found on dry land that was once part of the ocean floor. Pahoehoe lava is runny and very fast-flowing. The surface cools quickly and forms a thin, smooth skin with hot lava still moving underneath, which can twist and coil the surface to look like rope. Aa lava flows move more slowly and are not as hot as pahoehoe. Aa flows cool to form sharp chunks of rock, which can be as thick as 100 m (328 feet).

Pillow lava

Pahoehoe lava

Aa lava

### RIVER OF FIRE
In this Hawaiian-type eruption the lava streams down from the volcano into an area where it burns houses and adds a new layer of volcanic rock to the ground.

**ASH CLOUD**
Ash shoots high in
the sky in explosive
subduction volcanoes.
In a pyroclastic flow,
the ash cloud drops
and speeds down
the side.

**SPREADING ASH**
Present-day Santorini in Greece
(indicated by the red dot) was the site
of an eruption in 1645 BC. Scientists
believe that a 30-km (18-mile) high
column of ash spread over a large part of
the east Mediterranean area (as shown).

• VOLCANOES •

# Gas and Ash

A s magma rises to the Earth's surface, the gases mixed in
with it expand or swell and try to escape. These gases
sometimes contain carbon dioxide and hydrogen sulphide,
which are both very harmful to humans. In runny magma, gases
have no trouble escaping and cause mild eruptions with a lava
flow. Gases trapped in thick, sticky lava build up and explode
violently. These explosive eruptions fling clouds of rock fragments
and hardened lava froth called pumice several kilometres into the
air. Ash is formed during the explosion when rock and lava blow
apart into millions of tiny pieces. Falling ash spreads further and
does more damage than lava flows do, although a small sprinkling
of ash can add important nutrients to the soil. Sometimes the
wind carries clouds of ash right around the world, affecting
weather patterns.

**COVERED IN ASH**
Residents in protective masks walk down a street in
Olongapo City in the Philippines after the ash fall
from the 1991 eruption of Mt Pinatubo.

22

## MAURICE AND KATIA KRAFFT

French volcanologist Maurice Krafft and his geochemist wife Katia were responsible for some of the world's most spectacular volcano photographs. They witnessed more than 150 volcanic eruptions throughout the world and wrote many books and films. Their fieldwork often placed them in great danger, and they had to wear heat-resistant suits for close-up photography. Both died in 1991 while they were filming a pyroclastic flow from the eruption of Mt Unzen in Japan.

## PYROCLASTIC ROCKS

Small fragments of volcanic rock and frothy pumice fly into the air. Larger bombs or blocks, some the size of boulders, bounce down the side of the mountain.

## PYROCLASTIC FLOW

This rapidly moving avalanche of volcanic fragments and gases, at a temperature of 100° C (212° F), can rocket down the side of a volcano at speeds of up to 250 km (155 miles) per hour, destroying everything in its path.

**A DANGEROUS SPOT**
Volcanologists collect samples
of gases erupting from the
crater of Mt Etna in Sicily.

· VOLCANOES ·

# In the Field

Scientists who study volcanoes are called volcanologists. They observe the activity of a volcano so they can try to predict when an eruption might occur. Volcanologists often conduct fieldwork near the craters or on the slopes of active volcanoes where they collect samples of lava and gas and measure any temperature changes. They watch for an increase of ash and fumes erupting from the crater. Minor earthquake activity recorded on seismometers set up on a volcano's slopes can also warn volcanologists of a possible eruption. At Kilauea volcano in Hawaii there are observatories near the vent where scientists have spent years recording details of its day-to-day life. A study of this kind provides information about a particular type of volcano and helps scientists to forecast future activity. Not all eruptions are predictable, however, and some happen with no warning.

**ROBOT VOLCANOLOGIST**
This robotlike instrument called Dante
was designed to crawl inside the crater of
Mt Erebus in Antarctica
to monitor gas and lava.

## DID YOU KNOW?
Volcanologists use a special electric
thermometer called a thermocouple
to take a volcano's temperature.
Lava is so hot that a glass
thermometer would melt.

# VOLCANO WORKSHOP

In 1988, after nearly 40 years of silence, Galeras volcano in Colombia showed signs of activity. An international workshop for scientists was set up there in 1993 to research and monitor the volcano. These scientists did their fieldwork on the slopes and in the crater of Galeras. On 14 January one group was working in the crater taking measurements and samples of gases. As the group left the crater the volcano erupted, killing nine people and injuring five more. The explosion caused a 3-km (2-mile) high plume of ash and gas. The scientists had been careful but the volcano did the unexpected.

**Subduction zone volcano**
Galeras is a 4,270-m (14,006-ft) volcano. The crater is 6 km (4 miles) from Pasto, a city with more than 300,000 people.

**Collecting data**
Scientists take gas samples from the edge of the inner crater where three men died when Galeras exploded 16 days earlier.

## WORLDWIDE EFFECT

A powerful volcano can shoot huge amounts of ash, gas and dust upwards through the atmosphere and into the stratosphere where strong winds carry it to all parts of the globe.

Stratosphere

Atmosphere

## • AFTER THE EVENT •

# Under the Weather

Volcanic eruptions produce a variety of hazards and changes to the environment. After an eruption the local area may experience months of strong winds, heavy rain and mudflows. Clouds of fine volcanic ash blown into the air affect people's breathing. The engines of aircraft flying in the area can become clogged with volcanic glass, dust and ash. Gas and ash ejected high enough into the stratosphere can travel all over the globe causing spectacular sunsets around the world. Weather patterns change in some areas as clouds of sulphur-rich gases reflect the sun's rays back into space and the Earth below cools. This kills plants and crops and affects the animals that feed on this vegetation. In many parts of the world volcanic twilights occur as sunlight is reduced and the temperature drops, which produces long cold winters.

## FIREWORKS
Static electricity caused by colliding particles of ash and lava sparks off bolts of lightning that crack in a fearsome display over an erupting volcano.

## THE OZONE HOLE
This satellite picture shows the hole in the ozone layer. The hole gets bigger when damaging chemicals from volcanoes are erupted into the atmosphere.

## NIGHT AT MIDDAY
The ash that fell from the 1982 eruption of Galunggung in Indonesia turned daylight skies to night.

## THE YEAR WITHOUT A SUMMER

Dramatic changes in worldwide weather conditions followed the 1815 eruption of Tambora in Indonesia. Ash from the volcano shot into the stratosphere and was carried all around the world, which lowered temperatures in some countries. Summer frost and snow damaged food crops in parts of Europe and Scandinavia, causing widespread starvation. Unseasonable snowfalls also destroyed crops in the northeast section of the United States. The sky in this famous painting by British artist J.M.W. Turner shows the yellow haze caused by the volcanic dust that settled over Europe after the eruption.

Nevado del Ruiz

Armero

**MUDFLOW**
In November 1985 the eruption of Nevado del Ruiz in Colombia melted ice and snow, which caused a devastating mudflow. Armero, 50 km (31 miles) away, was engulfed in a 40-m (131-ft) wall of mud and ash, which killed more than 23,000 people.

• AFTER THE EVENT •

# Mudflows and Avalanches

Mudflows and avalanches can be triggered by volcanic eruptions and earthquakes. Explosive eruptions can leave volcanoes covered with a layer of ash, which becomes like thick, wet cement when mixed with water from melting ice or thunderstorms. The resulting mudflows, called lahars, start to move downhill, gathering speed as they go. Stones, boulders, tree trunks and building rubble are picked up along the way. These moving streams of mud are often more powerful than rivers of water and can kill thousands of people and cause enormous damage over a widespread area before the mud sets as hard as concrete. In an avalanche, ash near a volcano's crater can collapse and carry away part of a mountain. Snow and rock may become airborne and travel at great speeds, crashing from a mountain top to a valley below in minutes.

**MIRACLE RESCUE**
Survivors were found up to three weeks after the eruption of Nevado del Ruiz. Relief workers from many parts of the world arrived with emergency supplies to help the survivors. Here, workers wash the mud off a rescued child.

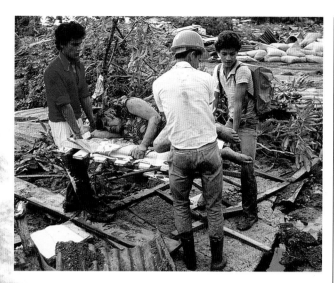

## LUCKY SURVIVOR
Fewer than 3,000 people survived the mudflow from Nevado del Ruiz, which destroyed the town of Armero.

## AVALANCHE!
An earthquake off the coast of Peru in 1960 triggered an avalanche from Huascaran mountain. Snow and rock fell 4,000 m (13,120 ft) and destroyed the town of Yungay six minutes later. More than 50,000 people were killed.

## STEMMING THE FLOW

Japan has a large population and 10 per cent of the world's active volcanoes. It leads the way in mudflow control. Scientists use television monitors and other measuring instruments to detect volcanic activity. Check dams such as these are used around the very active Mt Sakurajima. Steel and concrete slit dams, shown below, slow down and redirect flows of mud. Although the mudflows sometimes spill over the dams, people in danger have time to prepare or evacuate.

## WHEN A CALDERA FORMS
During mild explosions, magma rises to the top of the volcano's main vent.

## ERUPTING CALDERA
A cloud of ash and gas erupts from the caldera of Mt. Ngauruhoe in New Zealand.

## THE NEXT STAGE
As the eruption increases in strength the magma rapidly sinks back down to the top of the magma chamber.

## THE CLIMAX
In Plinian or Peléean eruptions, the activity climaxes and magma sinks below the roof of the magma chamber, leaving an empty space where it once supported the roof.

• AFTER THE EVENT •

# Craters and Calderas

Craters are the funnel-shaped hollows or cavities that form at the openings or vents of volcanoes. The simplest craters occur on the top of cones and usually have a diameter of about 1 km ($^6/_{10}$ mile) or less. Volcanoes can also form craters at the side. Small lava lakes occur when the lava is unable to escape, and it blocks the vent like a bath plug. Calderas are very large craters formed by an explosion or massive volcanic eruption. The magma chamber empties and can no longer support the weight of the volcano and the cone collapses. Calderas are often more than 5 km (3 miles) in diameter. The world's largest caldera is at Aso, Japan, and it is 23 km (14 miles) long and 16 km (10 miles) wide. When a volcano is dormant or extinct a caldera can fill with water to form a large lake.

## KILAUEA CRATER
Lava erupts from the crater of Kilauea volcano on Hawaii.

## CRATER LAKES

These lakes form when the main vents of dormant or extinct volcanoes are plugged with hardened lava or other rubble. Over many years the crater gradually fills with water from rain or snow. Shown here is Crater Lake in the United States. This lake is a caldera that formed when the summit of Mt Mazama collapsed more than 6,600 years ago. The small cone within the caldera is called Wizard Island.

### LIFE IN A CALDERA
Pinggan village is one of the many villages within the caldera of the extinct volcano Gunung Batur, in Bali, Indonesia.

### THE COLLAPSE
Once the magma support is removed, the top collapses into the magma chamber, and more eruptions can occur on the caldera floor.

### STRANGE BUT TRUE
On the Indonesian island of Flores, the volcano of Keli Mutu is well known for its different coloured crater lakes. Tiwoe Noea Moeri Kooh Pai is green, Tiwoe Ata is light green and Tiwoe Ata Polo is an amazing red colour.

*Discover more in* Volcanic Eruptions

**VOLCANIC PLUG**
This plug in Cameroon, West Africa, started as magma in the vent of a volcano. Over millions of years the magma cooled and hardened. The softer rocks eroded and left the plug exposed.

• AFTER THE EVENT •

# Volcanic Rocks and Landforms

**D**eep within the Earth the heat is so intense that the red-hot rock or magma is molten. This magma rises towards the surface through cracks in the crust, then cools and hardens to form igneous rocks. When these rocks cool slowly underground within the cracks they form intrusive igneous rocks such as granite. Intrusive rocks may appear on the surface when the surrounding softer rocks erode and expose amazing landscapes with landforms such as sills, dykes and plugs. Magma that erupts at the surface as lava and cools quickly becomes extrusive igneous rock. Runny lavas produce a rock called basalt, which in large quantities can flood an area and make basalt plateaus. Thicker, stickier lava can produce pumice, volcanic glass such as obsidian, and a light-coloured rock called rhyolite.

**ROCK WALL**
Most volcanoes are fed by magma that forces its way up through vertical cracks in the rocks. The magma can harden underground to form a wall of rock called a dyke. Erosion has exposed this dyke in eastern Australia, which is called the "Breadknife".

**HOT SPRINGS**
Hot springs form when water seeps down through rocks and is heated by magma or hot rock from below. The water then rises up towards the surface. This Japanese macaque enjoys a warm soak in one of the hot springs in northern Japan—a volcanic area near the boundaries of the Pacific and Philippine plates.

## DID YOU KNOW?

Diamonds originate in the mantle under extreme heat and pressure. Diamonds, such as this one embedded in volcanic rock called kimberlite, are pushed to the surface by rising magma.

## USEFUL VOLCANOES

There are many uses for volcanic rocks. Small amounts of ash can add nutrients to soil. Basalt and granite are useful building materials. The mineral sulphur grows around the vents of some active volcanoes. Sulphur is mined for use in manufacturing. It is added to rubber to make it last longer, and is also an ingredient in many explosives. Here workers carry baskets full of large sulphur crystals collected from around the vent of Kawah Ijen volcano in Java, Indonesia. This sulphur will be processed and mixed with phosphate to make a type of fertiliser.

## CAPPADOCCIA

This unusual volcanic landscape formed at Cappadoccia, Turkey, from lava eruptions of the now extinct Mt Erciyes. Wind and rain have eroded the volcanic rock into pointed formations.

# Surviving an Earthquake

When an earthquake strikes, beware of falling buildings and flying objects. To prevent building collapse and loss of life, engineers in many earthquake-prone cities follow strict rules when they repair earthquake damage or put up new structures. Many buildings are now designed to rest on reinforced concrete rafts that float when shock waves pass through. Existing buildings can be reinforced by cross-bracing walls, floors, roofs and foundations to help them withstand forces striking them from all directions. Walls and ceilings are strengthened with plywood in case of fire. Some areas have flexible gas lines that bend but do not break under pressure. Heavy furniture is bolted to walls to prevent it from flying around a room. Warning systems monitor stress in the Earth's crust, but earthquakes are still unpredictable and often much stronger than expected. In some areas earthquake-proof buildings have collapsed.

### BE PREPARED
Earthquake drills are part of the daily life of school children in Parkfield, California, in the United States. Part of the San Andreas fault system lies beneath this small town.

### SAFETY MEASURES
In this school, computers are bolted to tables, bookshelves and cupboards are attached to walls or fastened together. Windows are covered in transparent tape to stop them from breaking during a tremor.

### WHEN THE EARTH SHAKES
An earthquake alarm is attached to the school's propane gas supply. The alarm switches off the gas automatically if a tremor above 3.5 on the Richter scale rocks the building.

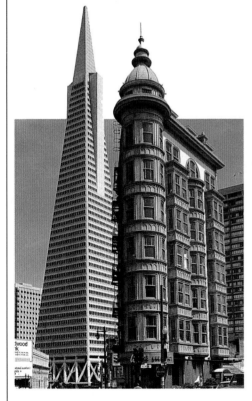

### TRANSAMERICA BUILDING
This rocket-shaped building in San Francisco, California, in the United States, is designed to withstand an earthquake. The base is built on a concrete raft that gives extra support.

### DROP!
When the teacher shouts "drop" each child crouches under the nearest desk. They link one arm around the leg of the desk to anchor it, and cover their head with both hands.

## LIQUID SOIL

Buildings constructed on loose wet soil, such as lake beds or filled land, are at a greater risk during an earthquake due to a process called liquefaction. When the ground shakes, the solid soil particles separate from each other and the soil itself becomes a thick muddy liquid. Buildings sink or fall over because they have no support. Cities such as San Francisco in the United States and Tokyo in Japan have building rules that require stronger foundations for new structures. The buildings pictured here toppled over during the 1985 earthquake in Mexico City, Mexico, as a result of liquefaction.

**TSUNAMI DAMAGE**
Indonesian fishermen try to save what they can from their house destroyed by one of the 12 tsunamis that struck East Java in June 1994.

• EARTHQUAKES •

# Tsunamis and Floods

Tsunamis, huge killer waves, are caused by a jolt to the ocean floor from an earthquake, volcanic eruption or landslide. Unlike a surface wave, a tsunami is a whole column of water that reaches from the sea floor up to the surface. It can race across oceans for thousands of kilometres at speeds of up to 800 km (496 miles) per hour—as fast as a jet plane. Such a giant wave might stretch for hundreds of kilometres from crest to crest and yet remain unnoticed as it passes under ships. A sharp rise in the ocean floor near a coastline acts as a brake at the bottom of the wave and makes it stop and rush upwards in a towering wall of water that crashes onto land. The power of the wave batters and floods the coast, causing enormous damage and loss of life. Tsunamis occur most frequently in the Pacific area.

**AS FAST AS A JET PLANE**
The spreading arcs of a tsunami, triggered by an earthquake in Alaska, spread quickly across the Pacific region. Seismic sea-wave detectors are in place throughout the Pacific area to measure the travel time of tsunamis and to warn populations in danger.

## GIANT SEA WAVES

In 1992 a mild earthquake, barely noticed, hit San Juan del Sur in Nicaragua. Minutes later the peaceful harbour was drained dry as if someone had pulled a giant bath plug and let the water out. Amazed at the sight, people flocked to the harbour to look. As they stared, a giant tsunami rushed in and swept people and buildings far out to sea. This three-part illustration is an example of how the water is drained in a harbour, then builds up speed and height before rushing back to the shore.

1½ hours
3 hours
4 hours
5½ hours
8½ hours
11½ hours
14½ hours
17 hours

**WAVE FORMATION**
The speed of a tsunami depends on the depth of the ocean. The wave gets higher and higher as it moves towards the shallower water near land.

**ETNA ERUPTS**
A column of ash, gas and lava shoots into the air during a 1992 eruption of Mt Etna.

**THE SLOPES OF MT ETNA**
An old illustration shows the lava flow from one of the four main volcanic vents.

• FAMOUS VOLCANOES •

# Mediterranean Eruptions

For more than two million years, earthquakes and volcanic eruptions have occurred in the area of the Mediterranean Sea along the boundary where the African plate meets the Eurasian plate. The Bay of Naples, in Italy, is the site of Mt Vesuvius, which erupted violently in AD 79 and destroyed the towns of Herculaneum and Pompeii. Pliny the Younger wrote the very first account of an eruption after observing the event. Since then, Mt Vesuvius has erupted numerous times. The last eruption was in 1944 but it is not known how long the volcano will remain dormant. Mt Etna dominates eastern Sicily and is Europe's largest active volcano. It has been erupting periodically for more than 2,500 years and regularly destroys villages and farmland. People continue to settle on its fertile soil. The last major eruption of Mt Etna occurred in 1992.

**ON THEIR DOORSTEP**
Mt Vesuvius looms above the modern city of Naples. When will it erupt next?

## DID YOU KNOW?
The 1944 eruption of Mt Vesuvius occurred during the Second World War. Glass-sharp volcanic ash and rock fragments seriously damaged aircraft engines.

## RAINING ASH

People fled the town of Herculaneum during the AD 79 eruption of Mt Vesuvius. Some ran towards the sea and escaped in boats but many perished when a hot surge of ash and gas covered the town.

## A GREEK TRAGEDY

The beautiful ancient Greek island of Thera (today called Santorini) in the Aegean Sea was destroyed by a violent volcanic eruption 3,500 years ago. The island was home to the Minoan people, a very wealthy and advanced civilisation. The eruption caused huge tsunamis and ash falls. These swept across neighbouring islands such as Crete, site of the Minoan capital of Knossos, where this vase was found. What was left of Thera was covered in more than 60 m (197 ft) of ash and pumice.

*Discover more in* The Digs

**DISASTER SITES**
This diagram compares the level of volcanic deposits that covered Herculaneum with the level that covered Pompeii.

Level of volcanic deposits at Herculaneum

Level of volcanic deposits at Pompeii

**PLASTER CAST**
In the 1860s, workers uncovering parts of Pompeii found holes in the volcanic rock left by the decayed bodies of the victims such as this dog. Scientists poured plaster into the holes to make models of the bodies.

• FAMOUS VOLCANOES •

# The Digs

T he sister cities of Pompeii and Herculaneum in Italy were destroyed when Mt Vesuvius erupted on 24 August AD 79. Pompeii lay 8 km (5 miles) from the volcano and throughout the first afternoon and evening hot pumice, ash and rock rained down onto the crowds of fleeing people. Herculaneum, less than 5 km (3 miles) from the volcano, had only small amounts of ash fall at first, but by midnight a pyroclastic flow of hot ash and gas followed by hot mud swept through the city, killing the residents. Early the next morning Herculaneum was buried under 20 m (66 ft) of volcanic deposits. Another surge of ash and gas killed the remaining residents of Pompeii and buried the city under 3 m (10 ft) of volcanic deposits. Over the years archaeologists have discovered bodies, buildings and many small objects that reveal the last moments of the doomed citizens.

## The First Volcanologist

From 32 km (20 miles) away, Pliny the Younger observed the AD 79 eruption of Mt Vesuvius. In AD 104 he described the event in two letters to his friend Tacitus, a writer and historian. This was the first recorded eyewitness report of a volcanic eruption. Pliny described such things as the Earth tremors that occurred before the eruption, the large amounts of ash and pumice, the low, hot ash flows, the many tidal waves and the total darkness of the sky. He also described a large column of ash shaped like a pine tree, which shot into the air. This type of volcanic eruption has since been named a Plinian eruption. Pictured here is a painting of a later eruption of Mt Vesuvius showing some of the same details described by Pliny.

**EVERYDAY ITEMS**
Artefacts such as this glass drinking cup were found unbroken beneath the rubble.

**RINGS ON HER FINGERS**
Nearly 100 skeletons, including this one nicknamed "The Ring Lady", have been discovered in boatsheds and on the site of the ancient beach of Herculaneum. These people died while attempting to flee from the gas and ash of the eruption.

## Strange but True
By studying skeletons, scientists can find out a person's sex, race, height and approximate age. Bones can also reveal the type of work a person did and the kind of food they ate.

**ROMAN COINS**
These coins were found still safe inside a soldier's money belt.

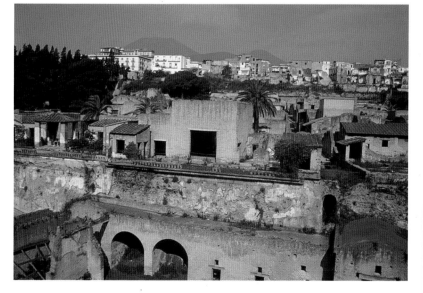

**HERCULANEUM TODAY**
The ruins of the town lie 20 m (66 ft) beneath the modern city of Ercolano. Mt Vesuvius can be seen in the background.

*Discover more in* Mediterranean Eruptions

## DID YOU KNOW?

Although the 1815 eruption of Tambora in Indonesia was a much larger and more violent eruption, Krakatau seized the entire world's attention because of modern communication networks.

**Over England**
The evening sky over London dazzled onlookers with beautiful colours. Waves raised the tides in the English Channel.

**Weather changes**
Volcanic dust circled the globe for several years and lowered the Earth's average temperature. Hawaiians noticed a white halo around the sun.

**Trinidad**
On the other side of the globe, in Trinidad, the sun appeared blue.

• FAMOUS VOLCANOES •

# Krakatau

In May 1883, ash, gas and pumice erupted from a volcano on the Indonesian island of Krakatau. The island is located in an unstable area where the Indo-Australian plate subducts under the Eurasian plate. The early rumblings from the volcano were just warm-ups before the violent explosion that blew the island apart on 27 August. The boom from the explosion, one of the loudest ever recorded, was heard 3,500 km (2,170 miles) away. Clouds of dust and ash rose 80 km (50 miles) into the air, circled the globe, and created many colourful sunsets around the world. As the volcano collapsed in on itself, giant waves called tsunamis rose more than 40 m (131 ft) high. These walls of water surged into 163 villages along the coastlines of Java and Sumatra, destroying them and killing almost 36,000 villagers. Floating islands of pumice endangered ships sailing in the Indian Ocean.

**NEARING THE END**
This nineteenth-century engraving was based on an old photograph taken in 1883, just three months before Krakatau exploded.

## CHILD OF KRAKATAU

When Krakatau erupted it collapsed in on itself and formed a 6.5-km (4-mile) undersea caldera. In 1927, observers noticed smoke rising from the caldera and within a year an infant island, called Anak or Child of Krakatau, appeared. It continues to grow and is fed regularly by gas and ash during its many mild eruptions. This picture shows Anak Krakatau as it appears today.

**In Calcutta**
Giant waves destroyed riverboats in this Indian city.

### AWAKENING GIANT
The volcanic island of Krakatau, in the Sunda Strait between the Indonesian islands of Sumatra and Java, erupted violently after more than 200 years of silence.

**In Sri Lanka**
Observers here reported that the sun looked green in the first few weeks after the eruption.

**Krakatau**

**In Alice Springs**
To people living in central Australia, the blasts sounded like rifle shots.

**The loudest noise**
The noise of the eruption was heard as far away as Madagascar.

**A year later**
Floating pumice from the eruption blocked some Indian Ocean shipping lanes up to a year later.

**In Perth**
The eruption caused a tsunami that destroyed this harbour in Australia.

*Discover more in* Under the Weather

43

# Iceland

Iceland is an island country that sits astride the northern Atlantic section of the mid-ocean ridge. The island provides scientists with an ideal place to study the ocean ridge above water. One part of Iceland is on the North American plate, which is moving westward, and the other part is on the Eurasian plate, which is moving eastward. As the island is slowly pulled in two, a rift or large crack is forming. Ravines and cliffs mark the edges of the two plates. Magma rising to the surface has created a series of central volcanoes separated by groups of fissures. As the area becomes more unstable, there is more earthquake and volcanic activity. Icelanders use the geothermal energy from their volcanoes for central heating, hot water and other electrical power.

**DRAMATIC DISPLAY**
Eldfell volcano gives a dramatic light show behind this church in the seaport town of Vestmannaeyjar.

## AN ISLAND ERUPTION
In January 1973, the seaport town of Vestmannaeyjar on Heimaey Island became the site of a new volcano called Eldfell. Most residents were evacuated, but for six months volunteers stayed behind to save what they could of the town.

### Lava flow
Residents armed with fire hoses sprayed water on the advancing lava that threatened to take over the harbour. They saved the harbour but not before the lava flow added another 2.6 sq km (1 sq mile) of new land to the island.

## DID YOU KNOW?

Iceland is the source of one-fifth of the Earth's recorded lava output. Scientists believe this is partly due to Iceland's position over an active spreading ridge and, possibly, a hotspot.

## LANDSCAPE OF FIRE

In 1783, the 5-km (3-mile) long Lakagígar fissure in southern Iceland began erupting huge fountains of lava and large amounts of gas and ash. The lava flow, one of the largest ever recorded on Earth, eventually covered more than 565 sq km (220 sq miles) of land. A deadly blue haze settled over the country and spread to parts of Europe and Asia. Nobody was killed by the lava itself, but Iceland's crops were destroyed and much of the livestock starved to death. More than 10,000 people died in the famine that followed. Since then, fissures such as the one at Krafla in northeastern Iceland have continued to erupt.

The craters of Lakagígar fissure

Krafla fissure

### BACKYARD VOLCANO

The crater of Eldfell glowed red as thick lava flowed down the side of the volcano and fiery ash rained down on the abandoned houses.

### BURIED IN ASH

Much of the town lay beneath a thick layer of ash. Here, volunteers clear ash from rooftops to prevent the houses from collapsing.

# Mt St Helens

The volcano Mt St Helens is one of 15 in the Cascade Range of the northwest United States—an area where the Juan de Fuca plate is subducting beneath the North American plate. On 20 March 1980, a string of earthquakes northwest of the mountain peak signalled the slow awakening of the volcano, which had been dormant since 1857. A week later, a small eruption shot ash and steam into the air. Groups of scientists arrived with instruments to monitor the volcano. By early May, a bulge developed on the cone. This indicated magma rising in the volcano's vent. The bulge grew bigger each day until a violent explosion, probably triggered by another earthquake, blew out the northern side of the mountain on 18 May. This caused an enormous landslide that devastated an area of 600 sq km (234 sq miles) and triggered mudflows and floods.

**BEFORE**
In early 1980 the beautiful snow-capped peak of Mt St Helens was surrounded by forests and lakes.

**AND AFTER**
The north side of the nearly perfect cone blew apart in minutes, causing one of the largest volcanic landslides ever recorded.

## PLINIAN PLUME
Minutes after the first explosion a second eruption produced a large Plinian column of ash and gas that rose to a height of 20 km (12 miles). This phase of the volcanic eruption continued for nine hours.

## LIKE MATCHSTICKS
More than six million trees were uprooted or flattened by rock blasted from the volcano. After a massive salvage operation to clear the logs, seedlings were planted to replace the forests.

## MUDFLOWS
Thick, sticky mud caused by melting snow and ice sped down the North Toutle River Valley into communities below.

## SWEEPING ASH

Millions of tonnes of ash shot 25 km (15 miles) into the atmosphere and the falling ash spread more than 1,500 km (930 miles) to the east. Ash fell like black snow in parts of Montana, Idaho, Oregon and Washington, and covered streets, cars and buildings. Cats and dogs downwind from the eruption turned pale grey from the ash that floated from the sky. But ash does not melt like snow and it had to be cleared. Most ended up in landfills.

## CITY IN RUINS

The earthquake struck at midday when many households were preparing their meals on hibachis—a type of open stove. As the buildings collapsed they caught alight and fire swept quickly through the city, killing thousands of people. All but one section of Tokyo was damaged by fire and the business district was virtually destroyed.

### WORLDWIDE RESPONSE

News of the devastating earthquake flashed around the world and many countries rushed to Japan's aid with relief supplies.

### • FAMOUS EARTHQUAKES •

# The Great Kanto Earthquake

The Great Kanto Earthquake shook Japan on 1 September 1923. The earthquake originated beneath Sagami Bay, Yokohama, 80 km (50 miles) south of the capital, Tokyo. The power of the earthquake registered a massive 8.3 on the Richter scale and the ground shook for nearly five minutes. A staggering 100,000 people died and more than 300,000 buildings were destroyed. The earthquake was soon followed by a killer tsunami, which swept people and their homes far out to sea. More deaths were caused by the many fires that broke out among the paper and wood houses. These building materials had been specially chosen to make the homes safer in an earthquake but instead they provided fuel for the raging flames. A second major tremor blasted the area 24 hours later and minor aftershocks followed in the next few days.

## JAPANESE QUAKES

Japan is situated where the Philippine plate and the Pacific plate are subducting under the Eurasian plate. This makes Japan the site of frequent volcanic eruptions, earthquakes and tsunamis. People in Japan feel Earth tremors every few weeks. Cities such as Tokyo have disaster teams ready to jump into action. Many people have prepared emergency supply kits with food, water and medicine, and most take part in earthquake drills. In October 1994, a major earthquake estimated at 7.9 on the Richter scale occurred in the ocean crust off Hokkaido, the northernmost island in Japan, causing many buildings to collapse (above). Three months later an earthquake estimated at 6.9 on the Richter scale shattered the city of Kobe. More than 5,000 people died.

### REDUCED TO RUBBLE
So great was the force of the earthquake that the floor of Sagami Bay split. At the seaport of Yokohama, south of Tokyo, most buildings were destroyed as well as the harbour and port facilities.

*Discover more in* Quake!

# Mexico City

An earthquake measuring 8.1 on the Richter scale struck Mexico City on 19 September 1985. As the Cocos plate subducted under the North American plate, it fractured or cracked 20 km (12 miles) down in the mantle. The vibrations to the ocean floor unleashed a tsunami and produced a surge of energy 1,000 times greater than an atomic bomb. The seismic shock waves travelled 350 km (217 miles) east to Mexico City. This city is built on top of a dry sandy lake bed of soft sediment or subsoil, which amplified the shock waves so much that many buildings collapsed. Some of the city's largest skyscrapers remained standing, but L-shaped buildings and those with large open foyers were badly damaged. The earthquake killed more than 9,000 residents, while 30,000 were injured and 95,000 were left homeless.

**SHIFTING PLATES**
Mexico City lies in an area where several plates meet.

**ON SHAKY GROUND**
Mexico City is built on the same dry lake bed as the old Aztec capital of Tenochtitlan. The area is surrounded by volcanoes and prone to earthquakes.

## SIGNS OF LIFE

Teams of rescue workers carefully searched through the rubble of destroyed buildings looking for survivors. They listened for sounds of life in the wreckage. Rescuers worked nonstop for days after the earthquake and saved more than 4,000 lives.

## A CLASH OF FOUR PLATES

The Nazca, Cocos, South American and Caribbean plates meet and interact along the eastern section of the Pacific Ring of Fire. Plate movement triggers a large number of earthquakes and volcanoes in some areas of North America, Central America and South America. Pictured here is Arenal volcano in Costa Rica.

## STRANGE BUT TRUE

A four-day-old baby boy survived for nine days buried under the rubble of a hospital. Here the miracle baby is lifted to safety by rescue workers.

# Californian Quakes

Many of the world's earthquakes occur along an edge where two lithospheric plates meet. The state of California in the United States straddles two such plates. Most of the state sits on the North American plate, which is moving very slowly. The Pacific plate, with the rest of the state, is grinding past the North American plate more quickly, and moving northwest. The grating movement of the two plates has made a weblike series of faults and cracks in the crust where earthquakes can occur. The San Andreas Fault is the most famous fault in California and slashes through the state for 1,100 km (682 miles). From time to time the rock breaks and moves along a section of the fault, and this can trigger an earthquake. Scientists record more than 20,000 Earth tremors in California every year, although most are slight and detected only by sensitive instruments.

Sacramento

San Francisco 1906

Oakland

Morgan Hill 1984

Loma Prieta 1989

Coalinga 1983

Parkfield

**STRANDED**
Many commuters were trapped when sections of the Californian freeway system collapsed during the Loma Prieta earthquake in 1989.

## DID YOU KNOW?
Los Angeles sits on the Pacific plate. San Francisco sits on the North American plate. Perhaps in a million years or so they will meet.

### THE STREETS OF SAN FRANCISCO
A major earthquake could strike California at any time. Movement along the San Andreas fault system could cause massive destruction in cities such as San Francisco and Los Angeles. Oil refineries, chemical and atomic plants, office towers, schools, hospitals, freeways, sporting arenas, amusement parks and residential areas would all be affected.

## SLIPPING PLATES

This map of California shows the San Andreas and other major faults, as indicated by red lines. Labels show the sites of earthquakes that have occurred over the past 100 years.

## SAN FRANCISCO 1906

On 18 April 1906, an earthquake measuring 8.3 on the Richter scale struck San Francisco. Huge buildings crumbled and massive fires burned out of control for three days as the main water lines were destroyed. People crowded into the streets searching for relatives and shelter. The Red Cross set up emergency food lines to help feed more than 300,000 homeless. The final toll was staggering. The city centre lay in ruins. More than 28,000 buildings were destroyed and nearly 1,000 people perished.

Santa Barbara 1925

San Fernando 1971

Northridge 1994

Los Angeles

Palm Springs 1986

Long Beach 1933

San Diego

## NARROW ESCAPE

A home and car are destroyed during the Northridge earthquake in 1994.

## EARTHQUAKE TRAUMA

A survivor tearfully surveys a building damaged during the Loma Prieta earthquake of 1989.

*Discover more in* Quake!

# More about Volcanic Eruptions

### AD 186 Taupo, New Zealand

One of the largest volcanic eruptions in history occurred in Taupo in the North Island of New Zealand. Although quiet for more than 1,800 years, the volcano is still considered to be active.

### AD 79 Mt Vesuvius, Italy

The cities of Pompeii and Herculaneum were destroyed in AD 79 when Mt. Vesuvius erupted. Until then, people did not know that the mountain was a volcano—it had been silent for more than 300 years.

### 1783 Lakagigar, Iceland

Lakagigar fissure erupted one of the largest amounts of lava in history. The fissure also erupted huge amounts of ash and poisonous gases. A blue haze settled over parts of Europe. The American Benjamin Franklin, living in France at the time, correctly blamed the unusually cold summer on the eruption in Iceland.

### 1815 Tambora, Indonesia

The eruption of Tambora is considered to be the most destructive volcanic explosion ever. More than 10,000 people died during the eruption and a further 82,000 people died of disease and starvation after the event.

1991 Mt Pinatubo, Philippines

1902 Mt Pelée, Martinique

### 1902 Mt Pelée, Martinique

After signs of increased volcanic activity, Mt Pelée exploded violently, destroying the beautiful city of St Pierre. A glowing cloud of gas and ash raced down the mountain towards the city below. More than 28,000 people perished in less than a minute. The only survivor was a prisoner held in a tiny dungeon.

### 1980 Mt St Helens, United States

The sound from the massive explosion of Mt St Helens travelled for less than 10 km (6 miles). It was muffled by the huge cloud of ash and dust. People watching from 18 km (11 miles) away could see the huge explosion but heard nothing at all.

### 1982 El Chichon, Mexico

More than 3,500 people were killed in this eruption. So much ash shot into the sky that it remained dark for 44 hours.

### 1991 Unzen, Japan

The 1991 eruption was predicted by scientists and most people were evacuated in time. Many of the 38 people who perished in this explosion were geologists studying the eruption and journalists reporting it.

### 1991 Mt Pinatubo, Philippines

After more than 600 years, Mt Pinatubo erupted. Large amounts of ash exploded into the atmosphere and fell over a wide area. People sifting through the ash found what they believed to be diamonds. The rocks were actually quartz crystals formed by the hardening of magma inside the volcano.

1994 Rabaul, Papua New Guinea

### 1994 Rabaul, Papua New Guinea

The 1994 eruption was the sixth to occur in the past 200 years. Due to a successful evacuation there were very few deaths. The city was covered in a 1-m (3-ft) layer of ash and large slabs of pumice filled the harbour.

# More about Earthquakes

1755 Lisbon, Portugal

### 1755 Lisbon, Portugal

This wealthy merchant city was destroyed by an earthquake estimated by later seismologists to be 8.7 on the Richter scale. Buildings collapsed, tsunamis pounded the waterfront and fires burned for six days. The damage on the North African coast was so heavy that many people thought there were two earthquakes. The Lisbon earthquake was the first to be studied by scientists.

### 1897 Assam, India

The Assam earthquake, with a magnitude of 8.7, is one of the largest ever recorded. For the first time instruments confirmed the three types of earthquake waves.

### 1960 Santiago, Chile

A series of earthquakes killed more than 5,000 people. The surface waves produced were so powerful that they were still being recorded on seismographs 60 hours after the actual earthquake.

### 1964 Alaska, United States

The earthquake measuring between 8.3 and 8.6 originated 129 km (80 miles) east of the city of Anchorage. The ground shook for nearly seven minutes. Massive damage occurred in the heavily populated south-central area and surface waves reshaped the coastline. Large cracks opened up in the ground and landsliding was common. Tsunamis

raced across the Pacific Ocean as far south as Antarctica.

### 1976 Tangshan, China

The earthquake occurred in a heavily populated area of China 60 km (37 miles) southeast of Beijing. With a magnitude of between 7.8 and 8.2 the earthquake was the most devastating to hit China in four centuries. The earthquake lasted 23 seconds but was followed by more than 125 aftershocks within 48 hours of the first tremors. The death toll was staggering. About 242,000 people were killed and more than 150,000 injured.

### 1988 Spitak, Armenia

With a magnitude of 6.9, the Armenian earthquake completely destroyed the town of Spitak, and nearly every building in the cities of Kirovakan and Leninakan collapsed. Thousands were trapped in the rubble. More than 25,000 people died, but miraculously, 15,000 survivors were rescued.

### 1989 Loma Prieta, United States

A segment of the San Andreas Fault moved and triggered a magnitude 7.1 earthquake in California. Much of the damage in the San Francisco area occurred to buildings constructed on the soft sediment of landfilled areas. Ironically, some of the landfill material used in the area was rubble cleared from the 1906 San Francisco earthquake.

### 1995 Kobe, Japan

More than 5,000 people died and 200,000 were left homeless in one of Japan's worst earthquakes. In 30 seconds a devastating earthquake destroyed the city of Kobe and the surrounding villages. Broken gas mains caused fires, which swept through the streets and the tile-roofed wooden houses. Firefighters were unable to stop the flames from spreading—water mains were broken and useless. Most people were still asleep in their beds but many early morning commuters were trapped or killed when expressways collapsed.

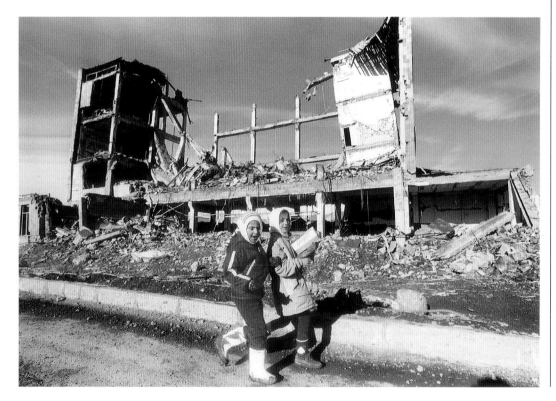

1988 Spitak, Armenia

# Index

## Picture Credits

(t=top, b=bottom, l=left, r=right, c=centre, F=front, C=cover, B=back, Bg=background)
Art Resource, 41tr (Borommeo). Auscape, 23tc (Explorer/K. Krafft), 15tr (J. Foott), 31tr (F. Gohier), 6/7c, 14br, 15tl, 24/25c, 27cr, 47tr (M. Krafft), 32br (W. Lawler). David Austen, 33tr. Austral International, 53tcr, 32tl (Colorific!), 52cl (IME - Sipa Press/K. Levine), 29tr (Rex Features), 53tr (Sipa-Press), 53br (Sygma/J.P. Forden), 53bcr (Sygma/L. Francis Jr, The Fresno Bee), 53cr (Topham Picture Library), 35tr (Nik Wheeler). Australian Museum, 33tl (J. Fields). Australian Picture Library, 38cl (Agence Vandystadt/G. Planchenault), 52/53b (A. Bartel), 54bl (Reuters), 22br, 36tl, 55br, (Reuters/Bettman), 29cr (Zefa/W. Janoud), 34bl. Black Star, 43tr (J. Delay), 46/47c (J. Mason), 46bl (R. Perry). The Bridgeman Art Library, 38bl, 41tc (Phillips, The International Fine Art Auctioneers). British Museum, 17cr. Bruce Coleman Ltd, 4bl, 32bl (S. Kaufman). Bruce Coleman, Inc, 47cr (J. Balog). Earth Images, 47br (B. Thompson). Fairfax Photo Library, 13tcr, 54cr (R. Stevens). Fratelli Alinari, 16cl. Gamma Liaison, 28bl (A. Suau). Fraser Goff, 46cl (J. Hughes), 25br, 25cr. The Granger Collection, 8br, 24tl, 38c,

42br, 48tr, 49tl, 55tl. Icelandic Photo and Press Service, 45tc (S. Jonasson), 11br (G. Palsson), 44tr, 45tr (M. Wibe Lund). The Image Bank, 20cl (L.J. Pierrce). Landform Slides, 31c, 41br. Mary Evans Picture Library, 48bl, 54tc. Megapress (Muroran Civil Engineering Office, Hokkaido Government), 29br. Minden Pictures, 20tl (F. Lanting). Mirror Syndication International, 50cl (British Museum/PCC/ Aldus). NASA, 24bl. National Archaeological Museum of Athens, 39br. National Geographic Society, 40/41c, 41c (O.L. Mazzatenta). NHPA, 38bc (A. Nardi). Pacific Stock, 30br (J. Carini). The Photo Library, Sydney, 51tr (G. Dimijian), 19tr (A. Evrard), 27tr (NASA/ Science Photo Library), 49tr (Sipa Press), 30tl (R. Smith), 21bcr (TSI/G.B. Lewis). Photo Researchers, Inc, 50/51c (F. Gohier). Robert Harding Picture Library, 21br (A.C. Waltham). Roger-Viollet, 49bc, 49cr, 49cl (Collection VIOLLET). John S. Shelton, 9br. Sonia Halliday Photographs, 40cl. Sporting Pix, 48tl (Popperfoto). Tate Gallery, London, 27br (Cat. no. N00499). Topham Picturepoint, 21cr.

## Illustration Credits

Andrew Beckett/Garden Studio, 28/29c, 28t, 44/45c. Sian Frances/Garden Studio, 5br, 34/35c, 51br. Mike Gorman, 18/19c, 18l, 40tl. Peter Kesteven/Garden Studio 38/39c. Mike Lamble, 32/33c. Kevin O'Donnell, 37r. Evert Ploeg, 42/43c. Oliver Rennert, 6tl, 8/9tc, 8l, 8tc, 9bl, 12/13c, 30/31c, 36/37c. Oliver Rennert and Ray Sim, 13cr, 14tr. John Richards, 2, 3, 4/5b. Trevor Ruth, 10/11c, 11cr, 14/15c, 20/21c. Stephen Seymour/Bernard Thornton Artists, UK, 5tr, 22/23c, 22cl, 23tr. Ray Sim, 16tl, 50tr. Kevin Stead, 26/27c, 26tl. Steve Trevaskis, 4tl, 16/17c, 17tr. Rod Westblade, 1, 29br, 37b, 52/53c, 53tc, endpapers, icons.

## Cover Credits

Auscape, Bg, FCbr (M. Krafft). Oliver Rennert, BCbr. John Richards, FCc. Stephen Seymour/Bernard Thornton Artists, UK, BCtl.